Maybe one day, you can look into the mirror and smile.
Maybe one day, you can go to bed and be at peace for a while.
Maybe one day, you will have all the riches you can imagine.
Maybe one day, you find the courage to forget what could've been.
Maybe one day, you will feel like you're enough.
Maybe one day, you can finally find love.
Maybe one day, you won't need to cry.
Maybe one day, you'll never give up
Please...try...

Maybe One Day

To be honest, I've always wanted to be a better person.
I always thought that maybe one day I could be more
than the trauma's I've experienced,
More than the pain of being alone and lonely,
Of finding out that people are less than they seem and
more than they perceive,
That we are never truly against each other,
But for ourselves...

I thought one day I could realize that
Heartbreak happens because one heart has to be saved
And that hurt people hurt people because at the end
We are all truly searching for our other puzzle piece
But will have to break and mold before we do
And that the image of the final product
Is seldom the clearest image
Of your desired lover and you

Laying here thinking of the past,
Your face pops up in my head.
All those times we smiled and laughed
Turn to breaking down by the bed…

We watched movies till late,
Danced and played,
Gosh… you were the best...

But now my room is silent and dark
With a heartbeat strapped to my arm,
Why didn't God take me instead…

I want to lose myself in the little moments

The ones where we laugh uncontrollably with friends
Over the smallest of jokes

The ones where I speed down the highway with only the
wind
And music in my ears

The warm summer days splashing around with my
family in the pool
Enjoying the few times we can smile together...

I want to lose myself in the little moments

The ones I will think back on at the end of my days
The moments that will truly make this life
Worth living

Writing in traffic
I sit with the red lights in my eyes
Flashing the memories that led me to this day.

I lost you, that much is true
But is there a word or saying
For a tongue-tied mind?

Usually, I wouldn't be able to get the words out
Usually, my mind would run and run and run
But with you…
I can't find the key to the lock
And for once, I'm a hostage in my head
Or maybe I always have been…

Unfortunately, I sometimes want to give up.
I know, I know, I have to work and grind to be
Where I want to be,
But when does it stop?
I'm always told there is no tomorrow,
So I'd better get work done while I still can...
I can work like there's no tomorrow,
But what would that work mean if there won't be a
tomorrow?
What's the reality?
What do you do when you face a hard truth
And a beautiful lie?
What do you do when you stand in your own way
By telling yourself lies?
Someone tell me, cause I've never been too sure...

Maybe it could've been you.
Maybe somewhere out there we lost ourselves
In the possibilities that life had presented us.
Maybe all it took was you taking a left and me, a right
To just be strangers.
We would've skipped the pain, the break,
The hurt and constant arguing,
The loss of a love we thought we were saving,
But the truth is that our path intersected at a single point
And we've been holding each other's hands,
Riding on trains going in opposite directions…

I'd like to think this life is mine.
I'd like to think I work for myself,
To provide for me,
That I am happy with myself.

I would like to pretend that I haven't dealt with mental
health issues,
That I haven't been heartbroken,
That I never felt alone,
Never felt lonely.
I'd like to think this is a life I can truly own for myself
But I'm not sure…
The moment I'll know is the final moment I'll be able to
cherish...

What does it feel like to fall out of love?

That fall, I always remembered the early moments

The tingles when we'd talk, and the butterflies
Every time the sun hit those eyes

The way my mind ran marathons over the thought of you

Tell me, did the same happen to you?

Did you feel the butterflies fly away?
Or did you hire an exterminator?

Did he numb those tingles, those moments when we
smiled
Like the world was ours

Did he fill the gaps of that heart I cherished like the
finest of treasures?

Are you happy without me now?

2 am and all I can do is think.
If I'm honest, I haven't slept for a few days.
I'm not completely sure why...
I have a home,
A family that tries their best,
I have food on the table,
Health to be proud of,
Opportunities knocking,
And a future that seems bright,
But for some reason,
Staying alone with my thoughts for those moments
before sleep
Keeps me from sleeping.
Makes me watch videos till I collapse,
Write to escape the skeletons in my closet and past,
Blast any music or noise to get the thoughts out
Though that usually doesn't last...

It's 2 am, is being awake really that bad?

The world never felt so small.
Traveling to see what there is to be offered,
The different people who aren't so different,
The different climates that are still the same.
Maybe being born in New York City jaded me to the world...
The skyscraping goliaths,
The hundreds of thousands of people,
Who speak differently,
Look different,
Act different,
But remain, family,
Maybe the world isn't boring.
Maybe I've just grown up with the world on a silver platter.

You were the first person to say you loved me.
You were the first person to promise you wouldn't hurt me.
You were the first person to ask about my past.
You were the first person to wipe my tears and hug me back.
You were the first person to want a life with me.
You were the first person to say you don't care about me.
You were the first person to say I'm the same as other guys.
You were the first person to say I'm a bad person.
You were the first person to say it'd be an easier situation if I died.

But it's still my fault, I guess…

Is it fair of me to look at you and think about our good times?
I think if I think about the good times,
This decision will be even harder to make.
I've always worn my heart on my sleeve,
But it seems like you've taken my whole arm,
Leaving me bleeding out without a way to replenish
Like a speeding car with a punctured gas tank,
I fuel my own demise.

It's been a long time since I've had my name called.
Phone dry, nightly cry
I'm alone. Well, lonely at least.
I never learned the essence of being human.

Of meeting others.

Building connections.

And some think its because I don't care,
But the truth is
I care too much

Sometimes knowing what could've been can save you years
Of wondering what the right decision was
Because a moment of pain and dread
Outweighs years of failed potential and heartbreaking toxicity

The fall breeze blows through and brings with it the
smells of a better time.
The pumpkin and heartwarming spices,
The food and smiles along the way,
The times when you were here with us,
Damn, I still remember those days…

The last time I felt this way, I lost myself for nights.
The four walls falling in,
My mind speaking loud,
Longing for human interaction
While wanting to stay alone.
Peace in the panic of solitude,
Shouldn't I be happy by now?

In a gloomy shadow of my mind
I meet a stranger, face hazy as the surrounding air,
Young, bright, and kind.

A juxtaposition of the very thing I wish I could be,
The very thing I wish I could see
In everyone around me.

We walk closer to the water,
Clouds overhead and stream laying still
Ripples near where we stood

If looks could kill...

Why can't I be like the shadow in my mind?
Why can't I forget the world?
Become more
And live my life

Why can't I finally be the shadow I am treated as
If I will be alone anyways in time

We're all the same. I think truthfully that if we were to
somehow compare to one another,
There would barely be a carbon difference between us.
We feel the same emotions defined by the same words,
Breathe the same air,
Learned that the worst of our days can get worse
But we smile all the same.
We laugh all the same.
We cry all the same.
We want the same thing,
To be Happy

There are plenty of questions in my head,
Plenty of answers I wish I had.

What would life be without the curiosities of a life
We want to have fully lived

And about a love

That we once thought would be the final attempt.

We pray for fewer struggles,
For something to finally work out
But who would we be without the struggles life throws
in our way?

Often, I look at the moon for some answers.
I know, I won't hear any response, but there is a
mystification
Staring at the glittery gold of the night sky

The vast nothingness that has more than I can even
imagine

When I look into the ever-expanding space around us
I peer into the future

The endless potential of the nothing I can make into
anything

Do you ever think of me?
I go out with friends, get a drink or two
Make it back home and only think of you

My heart sinks every time as I try to stay afloat

Maybe this time I won't

I sit here in silence
But my mind is the night sky on the Fourth of July,
Lights burning away at what remains of my peace,
I cannot sleep,
Cause if I do, I get nightmares about you,
About love and life,
Everyone's death,
Except for mine...

I can barely breathe, I promise I'm trying
You're out partying while I'm in bed dying
But my soul is still holding on
By a single thread I call hope
That maybe one day I will be enough
That maybe one day I will be in love
That maybe one day I won't fall apart
That maybe one day I won't need a reason to get out of
bed
And find a reason to start...

I am disappointed that what I need in life is love.
That is until I realize all of my studies, all of my reading
All of my work points to a single answer…
I am human.
I am an animal on a giant mass traveling hundreds of kilometers through space,
Space, the ever-expanding nothingness filled with more than I can fathom.
I was born to eat and reproduce
But with an extra catch,
A mind to ask why,
A mind to crave more,
A mind that battles every instinct I have,
In choosing my future over a lover,
Even though every lover chooses another over me.
The cruel reality is that there is no mysticism behind love,
There is no magic rule or secret potion,
There is no wishful thinking and praying.
Love is what we make of it,
Just as life is what we take from it…
My only issue is finding the difference...

I can feel you slipping away,
Like a boat untied during a storm
You gently float out to larger oceans
Towards a world of possibilities

I watch on, drenched in the rain and surrounded by
lightning
In peace

Cause though the waves may be rough on the way out
You will find what you need...

I grew up thinking love would be the cure to my
loneliness
Yet here I see myself unravel in the dark of these four
walls
Heart sinking like an anchor in the pacific
Reaching new depths unexplored.
No light, no technology
No person, no familiarity.
Just a warm crevice where life used to be
Once bright with the light of hope
Dulled by the recognition of broken dreams
Knotted rope
And the seams in between….

Please stay safe…
Your mind can be a scary place
So you don't have to go alone.
Talk to a family member, a friend
Talk to a professional, someone that will lend
A hand and an ear

You're strong
But even the strongest doesn't have to fight a war alone

On a rocket to the moon
I stare into the blue sky as it turns dark.
Surrounded by the silence of a roaring engine
An atmosphere-less cacophony of my heart.

It beats to the drums of the earth's ticking clock,
My only memory of home,
My only shot...

In a countdown, we land
But to my mistake
I left the fuel to return home
Back somewhere in your headspace

If you could leave a message behind,
What would it be?
What would be your final words,
Your legacy?

The most confusing parts of life always seem to happen at the best possible times.
Things work out even if they don't
And the sooner you learn the lesson,
The sooner your fears are conquered before they show

To be honest, I lie awake all night praying to one day
sleep.
I don't sleep because I'm scared of the nightmares I'll
see.
There's only so much a mind can take
Especially when the hell is one mine creates
And the four walls used to give me security
But now I look at them and question who I'm supposed
to be.

I'm not lying, I wish I could be me,
The younger me who smiled every day,
The one who saw hope and faith,
Smiles and wraiths around every corner...

I'm not lying, I'm tired of feeling lost, losing sleep
Jumping through every hoop, over every box
Like life is some video game you can beat

But every time I think I found a checkpoint
The nightmares tell me there is no point.

To be honest, I'm too tired, but I want to believe
That I can love enough to be enough to love
That I will do enough to finally earn some sleep
That I will finally learn there is strength in my blood
That I can and will be a better me

Maybe One Day...